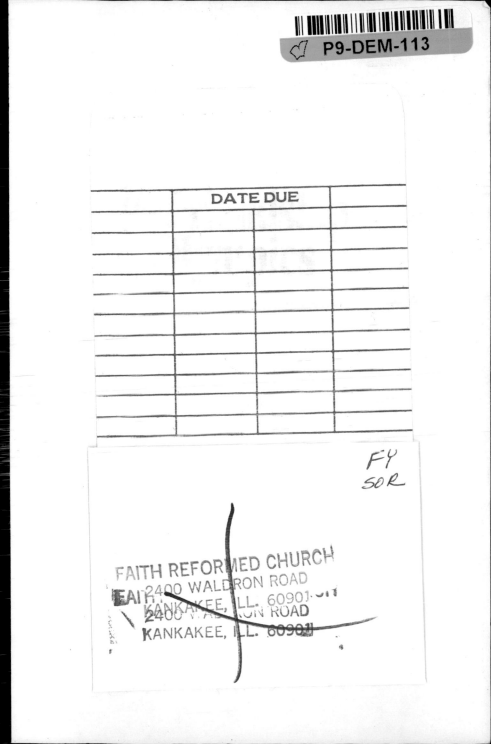

A YOUNG CHRISTIAN BOOK FOR BOYS

The Friendship Olympics

DAVID ALLEN SORENSEN

AUGSBURG Publishing House • Minneapolis

THE FRIENDSHIP OLYMPICS
A Young Christian Book for Boys

Scripture quotations unless otherwise noted are from the Holy Bible: New International Version. Copyright 1978 by the New York International Bible Society. Used by permission of Zondervan Bible Publishers.

Photos: Jim Whitmer, 10, 24; Jim Bradshaw, 16; Dave Swan, 30; Religious News Service, 38; Dale D. Gehman, 46, 68; Jean-Claude Lejeune, 52, 74, 98; Strix Pix, 80, 106; Gregory J. Larsen, 90.

Library of Congress Cataloging-in-Publication Data

Sorensen, David Allen, 1953–
  THE FRIENDSHIP OLYMPICS.

  Summary: A collection of stories and devotions
exploring the meaning and responsibilities of friendship.
  1. Friendship—Juvenile literature. 2. Boys—
Prayer-books and devotions—English. [1. Friendship.
2. Prayer books and devotions. 3. Christian life]
I. Title.
BJ1533.F8S65   1987   241'.676   86-32259
ISBN 0-8066-2248-2

Manufactured in the U.S.A.   APH 10-2430

   2   3   4   5   6   7   8   9   0   1   2   3   4   5   6   7   8   9

I thank God for parents who love their children like mine have loved me. My first book in the Young Christian series is dedicated with all my love to my mother and in memory of my father.

Thanks also to the fifth and sixth graders of my 1985 vacation church school class for dozens of great insights and ideas.

Contents

About This Book

In *The Friendship Olympics* we are going to push the boundaries of friendship to the limit. In a fun way, we will discover some of the powerful emotions that pass between friends.

Why should we look at the strong and unusual sides of friendship? Because there is a friend who pushed the boundaries of friendship all the way to the cross. And that friend is present "where two or three come together in my name" (Matt. 18:20).

Jesus Christ is that friend. His name may not be mentioned in every story in this book, but his presence is felt in each of the friendships that are part of "The Friendship Olympics." Watch and listen for him in these stories. He is in there. And as you read the Scriptures and prayers and action ideas that go with each story, you will see how Jesus is asking for a closer friendship with you.

Imagine Jesus standing on your doorstep asking for you: "Here I am! I stand at the door and knock. If anyone hears my voice and opens the door, I will come in and eat with him, and he with me" (Rev. 3:20). The person who answers the door turns and calls to you, "A friend of yours is here to see you!"

Jesus can be your best friend of all.

*"How did this whole thing get started?
I guess the Friendship Olympics started by accident.
On the other hand, maybe not!"*
—Barry

The Thinker

Barry's eyes followed his teacher's every move. She paced in front of the chalkboard like a circus leopard itching to return to Africa. But his mind was not on the class. When the last bell of the day had rung Barry would not remember one thing from this final class period.

Barry was a master daydreamer. He could travel vast distances in time and space in his mind while looking absolutely alert to all but his very best of friends.

Friends. Today, that was exactly what he was day-dreaming about.

A guy can do anything if he has the friends to help out, he thought.

He glanced around at the boys who sat in more than half the chairs in the room. He thought of all of them as friends in one way or another. Even some of the girls.

We could start a friendship club. Maybe even allow the girls to join. We could require every person to do things before they would be full members. Nothing dangerous—things like making friends with at least one lonely person, or really proving their friendship with the others somehow.

Barry looked more closely at the eyes of his friends as he wondered what heroic things they would be willing to do for him. Ben met his gaze and gave Barry one of those pay-attention-or-you'll-get-in-trouble looks. Barry glanced briefly at the teacher, then retreated back into his own thoughts.

We could call ourselves The Friendship Force. We could stick up for each other when the 9th grade bullies come around. We could give out tickets like the police, only ours would be given only to people who do friendly things. They would know The Friendship Force is watching. We could have—we could have—

Suddenly Barry knew that something was very wrong. All the other kids had their hands high in the air and faces that were turned toward him. He didn't understand it. The teacher hadn't asked a question. She had only been writing on the board.

The board. There, with Mrs. Shade pointing at them, were the words: "Raise your hand if you are paying attention."

"Mr. Jeffries," she said to Barry, "won't you be so kind as to stay after class today? Thank you very much."

The bell rang.

The others shuffled out more quietly than usual as they cast glances at Barry. Some seemed amused, others looked as nervous as he felt.

●

"That's an interesting thought, Barry," Mrs. Shade said. "Your idea about a Friendship Force is almost good enough that I don't mind your daydreaming—this time. But the problem with many clubs is that they tend to be too exclusive. Don't you think some of the class would feel left out if it were based only on your friendships?"

Barry couldn't believe his good luck. Mrs. Shade was actually in a good mood about all this.

"Barry, do you think you could come up with a way that we could all be a part of these ideas of yours about friendship?"

Barry's head swirled with so many ideas that he paused only a moment before saying, "How about if we have a Friendship Olympics?"

"Sounds interesting. What do you mean?"

"We would all enter stories about friendships in different categories," Barry replied.

"Categories?"

"Categories—events—like Oldest Friend, Youngest Friend, Most Friends, Longest Distance Friendship—things like that."

It was now Mrs. Shade's turn to pause for a moment.

"I like it very much, Barry. Write up the best categories you can think of this evening, and I'll add mine tomorrow before school. Then we'll pitch the idea to the class. I think it will really go."

"Great!" Barry said, as he slid out of his chair and moved for the door.

"And Barry," she continued, "I just want you to know that I know what your daydreaming look looks like now. You won't get by with it again."

"I understand," Barry said. "It used to be that only my best friends would know when I was daydreaming."

"Then let's just say I'm a new friend," Mrs. Shade said with a twinkle in her eye.

A teacher as a friend? Gary thought. *I'll have to think about that one.*

●

"Here are the categories, class," Mrs. Shade announced in class the next morning. "Most Time Spent with a Single Friend, Most Giving Friendship, Most Unlikely Friendship, Shortest Friendship, Most Improved Friendship, Longest Distance Friendship, Most Secret Friendship, Newest Friendship, Strongest Friendship, and Most Friends."

"Don't forget the Decathlon of Friendship," Barry piped up from his desk.

"Barry has added another category," she continued. "The Decathlon of Friendship is presented to the one who comes up with the best stories about friendship that cover all 10 of the categories I named.

"Now, remember this: The stories you share about friendship must be true stories from your own lives. We will spend the first half hour of each day for as long as it takes to hear all the stories in each category. Then we will vote on which story is the best for each event. Does everyone understand? Good. Let's have fun with this!"

Note to the reader: The following stories were judged by Barry and his class to be winners in his class's Friendship Olympics. Since there are more boys than girls in Barry's class, most of the winning stories deal with boys. Also, the class agreed that a proper Friendship Olympics can only be run with everyone on the same team. So everybody ended up on the winning team!

Mrs. Shade's prayer: Dear God, I hope I'm doing the right thing by going along with this Friendship Olympics idea. I know that if we aren't careful, feelings can get hurt. Help us to discover that looking for friendship doesn't have to be at the expense of others. Help us all to feel like winners at the end of the Olympics. Amen.

Action idea: Play along with the Friendship Olympics. As each chapter unfolds, enter your own stories next to those of Barry and his class. Play this with a friend as you read the book together.

"Two are better than one,
because they have a good return for their work:
If one falls down, his friend can help him up.
But pity the man who falls
and has no one to help him up!"
—Ecclesiastes 4:9-10

•

*"The next person who calls us twins
gets punched in the nose, OK?"*
—Steve

1st Prize:

Most Time Spent with a Single Friend

"This is your new brother," his mom had said.

*She should have said, "This is your new stepbrother,"
or "This is the guy who gets half of your bedroom," or
"This is the beginning of Round One in a great big
fight,"* Nick thought as he remembered meeting
Steve for the first time.

They hadn't hit it off too well at first.

For some reason that Nick never heard, Steve's
and his dad's belongings didn't come when they were
supposed to. Nick and his mom didn't need any
more furniture, so that was all right, but they had
to do without a lot more than that for a while.

17

"I've got to share *what* with him?" Nick had exclaimed to his mom.

"Socks, undershirts, and—"

"—and undershorts? Are you kidding?"

"Just for a few days, until the moving van gets here. He has blue jeans and a couple of shirts."

"You're kidding, right?"

"Nick, you know what an important time this is for Dick and I—and for you boys, too. We're going to feel like a complete family now."

"I might as well give him my toothbrush while I'm at it," Nick said with a frown.

"Money is tight in the middle of this move together," his mom said. "Otherwise we would buy the things we need. But you can keep your toothbrush. I didn't even know you knew you had one," she said with a chuckle.

Nick sat in silence on the couch, not fighting his mother's arm around his shoulders.

That night at supper Nick learned that he had more troubles.

"Pass the turkey to our guests," his mother told him.

He picked up the platter and passed it to Dick, who said, "You sound like we're here for a Sunday dinner and nothing more."

"Tonight," she replied, "you are guests. Tomorrow you can fight each other for leftovers like Nick and I do."

Dick helped himself to a drumstick, then passed the platter to Nick's mom.

He eats drumsticks! Nick realized with a start. *Oh, oh. What if Steve does too?* Nick's mother took the usual thigh, then passed the platter to Steve. Nick could see the last drumstick poking out from under the white meat. *Maybe he won't see it.*

Steve didn't hesitate. The other drumstick was soon his. Along with all the sliced dark meat.

The platter came back to Nick. White meat, white meat, white meat—nothing but white meat.

"It's going to be a long life," Nick muttered under his breath so only he could hear.

"What, honey?" his mother asked.

"I said, I think I'll go out in the kitchen to get the other thigh."

"Imagine that!" his mother said as he shuffled his chair back. "Four people under one roof who eat dark meat."

But the worst was yet to come.

The next day as Nick and Steve were getting ready to leave for school, Nick's mother called them together in the living room.

"Steve," she began, "you are new at this school today, so I want you to stick close to Nick. He knows where to go for classes, lunch, and to catch the bus home."

"I will," Steve said simply.

"And Nick, Steve doesn't have any friends here, so I hope you will share yours with him."

"I will," he replied.

"I want you two boys to be like twins, together all the time," she said.

19

Mr. Jennings used the same word to describe them when classes started that morning: "Nick Raines is going to introduce his twin to us this morning. Go ahead, Nick."

And the word caught on with his friends right away. "I'd invite you over tonight," Jerry said, "but I suppose your twin would have to come too, and we only have room for four to play pool, and Allen and Ben are already coming. You understand, don't you?"

And in the lunch line, Sheila said, "Let's see if the twins get exactly the same thing to eat. Isn't it funny that they don't look more alike?" Then she laughed at her own joke.

A month after the boys became each other's shadow—after Steve had finally gotten his own undershorts—they still hadn't gotten used to being called "twins."

Unfortunately, Steve used the word in talking to Nick one day in their bedroom.

"Jerry doesn't think the twins can beat him at shooting pool," he said. "But we used to own a pool table, and I think we could take him."

"Twins?" Nick said with eyes wide. "I don't ever want to hear that word again, especially not from you. I never wanted a brother, much less a twin."

"Oh, yeah?" retorted Steve. "I'm the one who had to leave my house to come and live here. Dad made me—"

"Made you? You mean you didn't want to come here?"

"Are you kidding? I had so many friends at my old school that I couldn't count them all."

"Are you as tired of following me around as I am of having you for a twin?" Nick asked.

"You bet!" Steve said. "And more."

"You steal drumsticks!"

"You mess up the toothpaste."

"You don't help with the dishes."

"You take paper from my notebook."

Nick looked at Steve for a long time. Steve stared back.

Finally, Nick said, "You're all right, Steve. I never knew you felt the same way about this as I do."

"You're not so bad yourself," Steve said with a wide grin.

"When you first came here I didn't think we would get along."

"Do you know what your mother almost did to me?"

"What?" Nick asked.

"She almost made me wear your undershorts! I would have run away first."

From then on Nick and Steve were almost always together.

Best of friends.

Almost twins.

Almost.

Nick's prayer: Dear God, I didn't used to have a brother at all. Now I have Steve. And I didn't used to

21

have a best friend. Now I have Steve. If you are the one who gives us all our blessings, I suppose I should thank you for Steve—even if he does take up more than his share of the bedroom. Amen.

Action idea: With what friend do you spend the most time? Figure out how many hours a week you spend with that person (in school and after school), divide that number by three, then pat that friend on the back today the number of times you end up with.

"How much more, then,
will the blood of Christ . . . cleanse"
—Hebrews 9:14

•

*"Blood is yucky and ishy
—but I'd do it again if I had to."*
—Greta

1st Prize:

Most Giving Friendship

"I have a story to tell," Gregory said one morning during Friendship Olympics time. "I think it might win for Most Giving Friendship, but I'm not sure if it's legal."

"What do you mean?" Mrs. Shade asked.

"The friend is my little sister."

"Sisters aren't friends," Rob said. "Sisters are—different—like a platypus. You wouldn't have a platypus for a friend, would you?"

The class laughed.

"Well, I'm a sister," Mrs. Shade said.

Rob immediately stopped grinning and folded his hands on his desk politely.

"So I'd be interested in hearing your story, Gregory," she continued.

"Well, the story really begins about three years

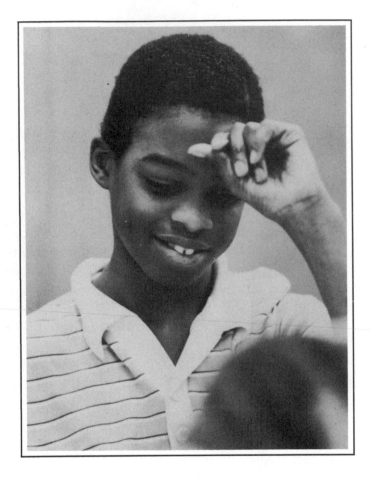

ago," Gregory said. "I was playing with a couple of friends in my basement. . . ."

•

Greta was two years younger than Gregory, but that didn't stop her from tagging along with him and his friends whenever possible. She was quiet and could sometimes be watching them without their knowing it.

This was a day like that. Hearing that Gregory and his two buddies would soon be going downstairs to play, she had crept down first and slipped into the closet under the stairs.

Soon she heard the creaking above her head as the boys came down, closing the door behind them.

"Get the cards," Chris said in a voice that sounded like he didn't want to be heard by anyone upstairs.

Greta peeked out the crack in her closet door and saw Gregory pull several shoeboxes out from above the furnace. Each fit neatly between the boards in the unfinished ceiling.

"Treasure!" Laine said, rubbing his hands together.

Gregory tossed the boxes onto the spare bed in the far end of the basement. Then the boys began pulling out stack after stack of baseball cards.

"Let's count them all again now that we have the new cards that you got from your uncle," Chris said to Gregory.

"We don't have to," Gregory replied. "These are in stacks of 100s, and I know how many new cards Uncle Pete gave me."

Gregory continued to lay the cards out in piles, then announced: "We have 1,537 cards now."

"And to think that we only had 500 when we combined all our collections last year," Chris said. "Wow!"

"They belong to all of us now," Laine said. "It would be impossible to sort out whose are whose now, wouldn't it?"

"That's right," Chris said. "It would be impossible."

"So I think we need to make a pact," Laine continued.

"What's a pact?" Gregory asked.

"You know—an agreement—a promise."

"About what?"

"That nobody in the group will do anything with these cards without the permission of the other two guys."

"I think he's right," Chris said. "Do you guys know how much these cards are worth?"

"Plenty," Gregory said. "We have cards going back to the old Washington Senators and a lot of other good stuff."

"So let's make a blood pact," Laine said as he pulled his pocket knife from his pocket. Then he flipped open the smallest of the two blades.

"Blood?" Gregory asked. "But—"

Just then, hearing the word *blood*, Greta cringed in the closet, shifting her feet and making a noise.

In just two seconds the boys were standing over her with angry expressions.

Greta hated blood. Gregory knew that. She hated seeing her own blood, she hated watching Sandy pick her scabs in class until they bled, she hated watching bloody TV shows, and she even hated looking at a bloody pound of hamburger until it had been cooked. Greta really hated blood.

"I won't tell where you hide your cards," Greta said, though you couldn't tell if she meant it by looking at her.

"You're right," Laine said, "because you are going to be in the blood pact with us."

Greta screamed once and then fainted.

●

We were never really going to cut anybody, Gregory thought as he lay in a hospital bed remembering that day with a smile. Poor Greta, she never really knew that for sure. Laine had just been acting tough.

A nurse in the usual white uniform entered his hospital room and said, "Gregory, it's time to go. We'll stop and see your family on the way, OK?"

"Sure," he replied.

"This isn't serious surgery, you know," the nurse continued.

"I know," he said. "But I've never had any kind of surgery, so it's a little scary."

"Sure it is," she said. The nurse helped Gregory into the wheelchair and said, "Just enjoy the ride, friend."

Poor Greta hates to be in a hospital at all. It was great of her to even come.

27

"Do you know why I didn't go for the surgery yesterday?" Gregory asked.

"Nothing serious," the nurse replied. "You happen to have an unusual kind of blood and, even though we don't expect any problems, we couldn't do the surgery until we had enough of your kind in our blood bank."

"Where did you find my weird blood?"

"It runs in the family, Gregory."

Dad always said we had the same kind of blood. Gregory thought. *I didn't realize that it was so unusual.*

"Hi, Greg," his father said as Gregory was wheeled into the surgery waiting room. "Nervous?"

"Sure," he replied.

"Well, you'll be out in a jiffy. Shouldn't be any trouble at all."

"But think of all your blood that will go to waste if I don't use it," Gregory said, enjoying the pained expression on Greta's face as he said it.

"They didn't want my blood," his father said. "I had malaria when I was overseas. If you got my blood you'd also get sick with malaria. It's in there forever even though it doesn't hurt me anymore."

"And my blood was the wrong type," his mother said.

"Then where on earth—" Gregory began.

Greta said quickly, "I don't even want to talk about it. It's gross."

"You?"

"Just call it a blood pact, Gregory," Greta said.

28

As expected, the surgery went well. Gregory never needed Greta's blood. But he never forgot the blood pact.

Greta's prayer: Lord Jesus, help Gregory get through his surgery. If he needs more blood, make me brave again. And Jesus, I don't think I would have done it if I didn't remember that you once gave your blood to help others too. Thanks. Amen.

Action idea: Make a list of the 10 best things a friend could give to another. If you could wish one thing for your best friend, what would it be?

"When Jesus saw him lying there and learned
that he had been in this condition for a long time,
he asked him, 'Do you want to get well?' "
—John 5:6

•

"I can't call it anything except a miracle!"
—Mark

1st Prize:

Most Unlikely Friendship

It was very unlikely that Rick and Mark would become friends.

Mark had cerebral palsy and went to a special school for kids who were handicapped. Rick had a reading problem but he still went to the school down the block.

Rick's sports included basketball, football, baseball, bicycling, swimming, and about six others. Mark was more interested in trying to get the muscles of his legs to work well enough to raid the refrigerator without anyone's help or to be able to play practical jokes on someone.

In so many ways the two boys were very different, but it seems that sometimes opposite kinds of people become friends.

The one thing that they shared together was that they went to the same church. They were in the same class in Sunday school, and both of them went every summer to vacation Bible school.

"I saw a bat fly into that crack in the wall up there," Mark said, pointing with a wobbling finger in the general direction of where the wall met the ceiling in the long hall.

"What did you say?" Rick asked. He stopped next to Mark's wheelchair on his way to the boys' bathroom.

"A bat just flew into that little crack."

"Where?" Rick asked, his voice rising a little.

"In that crack next to the ceiling," Mark said still pointing at a 30-foot area.

"There isn't a crack up there big enough for a bat to fly into, Mark," Rick said in a tone that sounded like Rick's mother telling Rick something he should have known.

Then Rick went into the bathroom.

When he came out, Mark pointed once again to the same general area and said, "Two more bats. That makes at least three. And who knows? We may have found the bat cave where a hundred of them live."

"Bat cave? I'm not stupid—I read Batman comics too. We have a bat cave in this church? Right," Rick said sarcastically.

"Or it may be the way the bats get in from the outside," Mark said.

Rick looked again at the narrow crack running the distance at the end of the hall near the ceiling. "I'll leave you with your bats now," he said.

"Wheel me outside, will you?"

"Outside?"

"Why not?"

"Because our parents will be done with choir practice any minute."

"We'll hear them when they're done. Let's go!" Mark said somewhat impatiently.

"Do I have to go because of the bats? I'll take you outside if you promise you won't laugh at me for falling for your bat gag. I don't, you know."

"Let's just go out, then, to look for the big dipper in the stars," Mark said.

"All right."

Outside, Mark said, "Let's look for the stars from over there. It's a better view. Who knows? We may even see a few bats—"

Mark never looked at the stars at all. But he saw what he was looking for. Stretching his right arm as slowly and still as he could, Mark pointed to the brick wall and said, "See? Bats going in and out of the church."

"Looks to me like they're flying at the wall and then turning away or just landing on a brick."

"But look closer."

"So?"

"Don't follow all the bats with your eyes. Watch just one. See what it does."

"It disappeared!" Rick exclaimed.

33

"It went to church—the hard way."

"But that crack isn't any bigger than—"

"—than the one inside in the hall."

Rick wheeled Mark back to the hallway and they both waited, looking at the top of the wall. People who came down the hall to use the bathrooms looked at them with strange expressions.

"Finally, there's a bat!" Mark said excitedly.

A single bat came out of the wall, flew in a single tight circle, then flew back at the crack and disappeared.

"Hey, Mark, what do you think of that?" Rick asked, then quickly added, "Sorry. I guess I didn't take you seriously."

"A lot of people don't take me seriously," Mark replied.

●

A month later, the church newsletter came to Rick's house in the mail. As usual, Rick didn't even look twice at it as he saw it sitting on the kitchen table.

But that evening at supper Rick's father said, "Are you interested in helping a friend?"

"What do you mean?" Rick asked.

"Isn't that boy with cerebral palsy at church your friend?"

"Yeah, I guess he is—"

"Well, you can help him if you want to."

"How?"

"The church is looking for people to help Mark with a new kind of therapy to help him walk."

"I thought he'd always be in a wheelchair."

"It looks like he has a chance if this new treatment and training works."

"Yeah, I'd be interested. But what do I have to do?"

"The church newsletter says to call the church office. Why don't you call in the morning before school?"

Rick called.

So did dozens of other people within a week.

Mark's mother and father worked with the volunteer coordinator to put together a weekly schedule that included everybody who had offered to spend time with Mark.

"What do I do?" Rick asked the person who called to tell him when he was supposed to come.

"We'll tell you when you get here," was the answer. "And more important, we'll *show* you. The things you *do* may help Mark to walk some day."

"Have you ever gone downhill skiing?" Mark asked Rick when he arrived at Mark's house.

"A few times."

"Well, you're going to help *me* ski too!"

Rick had enough respect for Mark after the bat gag that turned out to be true, that he didn't know what to say at first. He figured Mark would find a way to ski, if anyone could.

The volunteer who was training people in what they were supposed to do explained the details of what Mark was talking about.

"We strap Mark into the boots and skis, then take him for a walk," she began.

"I thought we were trying to help him walk *some-day*, not *today*," Rick said.

"The boots and skis give his ankles and legs strength that they don't have on their own."

"With the skis on, I can almost walk already!" Mark exclaimed.

"And with practice, we hope that some day he will walk on his own," the woman said.

"And ski," Mark added with a smile.

"He probably will," she said. "But for now, the key is that he practice and get into a pattern. In fact, that's what we call this therapy—*patterning*. Mark's brain and legs are not working together as well as they should, so we are teaching the legs a pattern. Mark's doctors say that the brain may just learn the pattern too."

"So Mark is walking first and learning *how* to walk second, right?" Rick asked.

"That's about it," she answered.

"That's just like a wise-guy, to do everything backwards," Rick said laughing. Mark grinned.

But it wasn't easy. At first, Mark struggled with every step. The skis seemed too heavy. Everything was too awkward. Mark could have asked to quit and the whole army of volunteers would have understood.

But he kept at it.

After months of struggle, Mark was able to walk smoothly, holding only one helping hand.

A few months later, he walked for the first time without assistance—no helps except the skis themselves.

Soon he was timing himself in the 50-foot dash along the carpet in the basement.

Mark is walking now without the skis. Rick walks with him often. Slowly. Now, Mark helps Rick with his reading problem. They can't figure out why Rick sometimes sees letters out of order or words in the wrong place. But Mark figures that if he and Rick simply read together out loud maybe Rick's brain will one day catch the pattern.

Who knows? Stranger things have happened.

Mark's prayer: It's a miracle, Lord. I can walk. We prayed for this to happen. We wanted you to come and help me, but instead you sent a bunch of people who could help and become my friends. It's great that you found an even better way of helping me than we had dreamed for. Thank you, God.

Action idea: Spend an hour pretending you don't have any arms. Find creative ways to do things that are usually easy but are now hard. And ask people for help if you need it. Wouldn't you help them if it was necessary?

"But God chose the foolish things of the world
to shame the wise; God chose the weak things
of the world to shame the strong."
—1 Corinthians 1:27

•

*"Have you ever met anyone who was 90 years older
than you are? I have."*
—Adrian

1st Prize:

Shortest Friendship

"I met Stuart only five days before he died," Adrian said simply. She didn't even try to hide the tears.

Rob, sitting in the corner desk by the door, slid down in his chair and tried to look unimpressed. *How could she even remember his name after only five days?* he thought.

"Stuart died only 10 days before his 103rd birthday," Adrian continued.

Oh, come on! Rob almost said out loud. *There should be rules about these friendship stories. How can someone make friends with someone that old? He must have been almost—*

"He was exactly 90 years older than me."

"That's quite unusual," Mrs. Shade remarked. "Why do you call him a friend instead of just someone you knew?"

She's on my side, Rob thought.

"Because of the gifts," Adrian answered. "We gave each other a special gift. Something only a friend would give. Let me tell you about it—"

•

Adrian's church had a great youth worker. His name was Peter Jones. And Peter had terrific ideas for things kids could do. Like the Adopt-a-Grandparent Program.

For three months Adrian and the others in the program spent one hour a week at a nursing home. Each of the kids chose an elderly person from the list of those who didn't get many visitors.

"I'll take Ella Miller," Susan said. "My grandma who died was named Ella."

Adrian glanced at the sheet and noticed that near the bottom was a man listed as 102 years old. "Is this man really that old?" she asked the head nurse.

The nurse looked at the list, shook her head, and said, "No—I mean yes he is that old, but he shouldn't have been put on this list. Sorry, you'll have to choose someone else."

"Why? Does he have enough visitors?"

"Hardly any," the nurse replied. "But he's so deaf that it doesn't do any good to talk to him."

"But I never knew my own grandfathers," Adrian said, "and he's the only man left on this list. Please, can I try to talk with him?"

"You can try, but I'll have another name for you next week, another gentleman. OK?"

"OK."

Stuart's room was number 102, right next to the cafeteria. The oldest residents were always given rooms on the main floor. Room 102 was special because it was always offered to the most senior resident. Later, Adrian found out that Stuart had very proudly moved into the room at age 99.

Adrian stood at the door of his room and wondered what to do. *Is he so deaf that he won't hear a knock? Wouldn't it be rude just to walk in?*

"Jusht waalk in," said a slurred voice behind her.

Adrian turned to see a beautiful woman with the fairest skin and blackest hair she had ever seen.

"Do you think I should?"

The woman's head fell to one side momentarily, but she lifted it again gracefully, smiled, and said, "Stu willl loove to seee you." Then she twisted a small black lever by her right hand and her motorized wheelchair moved down the hall. "Bye," she called over her shoulder.

I wonder if I should call him Stu or Stuart or—but he's deaf, isn't he? Adrian took a deep breath, turned the door lever, and walked in.

Inside, nothing moved.

I thought they said he'd be in his room, she thought.

The furniture was not like what you would find in a hospital, although that's what the room's walls and floors and smell reminded Adrian of. There was an old bureau with a spotty mirror above it, a rocking chair on a throw rug, an old chest that looked like

41

it might have carried an immigrant's belongings on a ship, and a tall, black—

Someone was sitting in the black chair looking right at her!

His eyes aren't moving. He's dead, Adrian thought as panic moved up her throat.

Stuart blinked through the thick spectacles.

"Hello," she said. "I'm with the Adopt-a-Grandparent Program."

Silence.

"I'll be spending an hour with you today."

Silence. Blink.

Adrian moved closer, with her hand outstretched.

Stuart remained motionless as she approached, sitting tall in the high-backed, old fashioned wheelchair next to his bed.

Then he flinched. Violently.

"Oh, I'm sorry!" Adrian said quickly. "You didn't see me until now, did you? They didn't tell me your sight wasn't so good."

She reached out for his hand—his trembling hand—and took it in a gentle handshake. Stuart reached over with his other hand and patted her hand, almost as if he were trying to comfort Adrian from a fright.

When she began to remove her hand, he held it even more tightly.

"You want to hold my hand, right?"

Stuart smiled kindly.

"You are not the regular nurse, are you?" he asked. Stuart's voice was too loud, with vowels that sounded funny.

Adrian repeated as loudly as she could without yelling, "I'm with the Adopt—"

"You are a child, maybe. A girl like my pretty Lisa."

"I'm going to spend an hour with—"

"Lisa is dead now, they tell me."

Adrian was silent.

"But that was a long time ago."

For a full minute they just held hands. Stuart's fingers never ceased moving over Adrian's hand.

The creases in Stuart's hands ran deep, but the surfaces of skin were surprisingly smooth. His hands were alive and aware.

After a while, he said, "I can't hear, you know."

"I know," Adrian said softly.

"And I can't really see anymore, either."

Adrian squeezed his hand reassuringly and said, "It doesn't matter to me."

"I don't remember if anybody in my family is still around. Are you a great-grandchild or something?"

Adrian didn't hesitate. She took both of his hands to her face, then nodded. The hands understood. To Adrian, that made the adoption legal. It didn't seem dishonest at all.

Stuart smiled broadly.

"I have some treasures in my top drawer."

She had been kneeling on the tile floor and was glad for the chance to stand up.

In the top drawer of the bureau she found loose pictures, clippings, old jewelry, a deck of cards, various keys on rings, and assorted objects that were not as easy to identify. She took a number of these back to her "grandfather," sat on the edge of the bed, and placed an oddly-shaped clock in his waiting hands.

"I took it from the cockpit of my biplane at the end of the Great War, in 1918. This clock only needs to be wound once a week. Isn't that amazing?"

Adrian looked down at her digital alarm watch with the stopwatch mode. She would change the battery every few years and might adjust the time only once or twice during that time. *What will people find amazing when I'm 102 years old?* she wondered.

The other items included a small canister of reusable ivory toothpicks—yellowed with age, a rubber stamp bearing the insignia of the company Stuart had founded after the Great Depression in the 1930s, an empty recipe box that he had made of fine wood for his wife, and a framed greeting from the president of the United States on the occasion of his 100th birthday.

Adrian placed each item into the waiting hands and was pleasantly surprised at the detailed memories they sparked.

"You must take one of these with you now. It's time for my nap."

Adrian took his hands once again to her face. She shook her head. The heads understood, but he stroked her hair once gently, then said, "Please," very quietly.

Sensing her uncertainty, Stuart said, "The clock is very old—like me. Take the clock."

She replaced the other items in the bureau, but tucked the clock into her backpack with her school books. Adrian knelt once again at Stuart's feet, held the hands of the pilot, businessman, and husband, then she kissed those hands that had communicated so well.

"Come again soon," he said.

"Next week," she replied. "I'll come every week."

•

"He died five days later," Adrian said to the class

From the corner of the room, Rob said, "You told us you both gave each other gifts. What did you give him?"

"He gave me a clock from his past," she replied, "and I gave him my time."

Rob's prayer: Lord, I don't have as much patience with older people as Adrian does. But give me another chance to be with someone like Stuart and I'll try to be a better listener. Amen.

Action idea: Does your church have an adopt-a-grandparent program? If not, who would you need to talk with to get one started?

"Dear children, let us not love with words or tongue
but with actions and in truth."
—1 John 3:18

•

*"I learned that you can talk about getting someone
to be your friend, but in the end it's better
to make yourself his friend.
It's a lot better."*
—Barry

1st Prize:

Most Improved Friendship

Last fall Ben was the only new kid in the class. At first the other students were content just to let him be quiet. But as fall turned cold and the first snow of winter fell, Allen, Rick, and Barry decided that he really needed to loosen up and be a part of things.

"We think we can help you to make some friends in school," Allen offered one day after all three had gathered around Ben. "You can start with us."

"I have friends," was Ben's curt answer.

"What? Do you have secret, little, make-believe friends like my four-year old sister that we don't know about?" Rick asked.

The three who knew Rick's squirrelly little sister laughed.

"They all live in Pennsylvania. They're the best friends in the world," Ben replied.

"So you don't need us," Allen said.

"You said it; I didn't," Ben replied. Then he turned his back and walked down the hall.

The three boys watched him go, shock registering on all their faces. Before Ben had even turned into the classroom, the shock had turned to anger.

Two days later, the three buddies were coming out of band carrying their instruments when they met Ben at his locker.

"We talked to Mr. Lippitz for you," Barry said, "and he said it isn't too late for you to learn a band instrument like us."

"Yeah, you'd be perfect for the dingaling—I mean the triangle," Allen added.

Before the boys could laugh at their own teasing, Ben said, "I take private cello lessons."

After a pause, Rick said, "Do you have to be a private fellow to study private cello?"

Now the three burst into laughter. Once again, Ben turned his back and walked away.

Over the next weeks, Ben refused to join Boy Scouts, the youth group at church, and anything else that the boys threw at him.

One day Barry, Rick, and Allen were shooting baskets at the YMCA. The basketball leagues would begin a week later.

"Mr. Griffin," Rick said as he saw the assistant director approach, "are we all going to be on the same team again this year?"

"As usual," he replied. "But this year I'm putting two other guys with you, one who needs a little help and one who's a real ace."

"What are their names?" Allen asked eagerly.

"Here comes one of them now. He's a new kid. See if you can make him feel at home."

It was Ben.

"Hey, Ben, we hear you're going to be on our team this year," Barry said.

"Mr. Griffin is trying to talk me into it, but I told him I'm already a member of the best team back where I used to live."

"It's a long way to go for games," Barry replied. With that, Barry dribbled the ball once behind his back, once between his legs, then scooped it up and shot it way over the backboard. "I finally missed one," he said as he snapped his fingers.

Rick winked at Allen and said, "Gee, was that six or seven in a row?"

Mr. Griffin caught the rebound on his way back to talk with the boys.

"So how about it? Do we have a new member of the Muskets for this year?" he asked.

"But I'm on the Buckets back in Pennsylvania already," Ben said as he turned his back on them all one more time.

A frown came over Barry's face, then a smile.

"I'm on the Buckets then too," Barry said.

Allen and Rick looked quickly at Barry as he spun around, then each said, "Me too!"

"What?" Ben asked as he turned back with a puzzled expression.

"Ben," Barry replied, "we've been trying to get you to join us for a long time. Maybe we've been doing it all wrong. So today we're going to join you."

"Sounds like we have a new team, Ben," Mr. Griffin said, "as long as that's all right with you."

"Sure. I guess so—"

"Then it's settled. By the way, Ben, your dad said you should stop by his office before you leave."

"OK, Dan," Ben said.

The other three boys looked a bit confused.

"And Ben, we'll see you on the racketball court Sunday night, right?"

"You bet!"

"How do you know Mr. Griffin well enough to call him Dan?" Barry asked after Mr. Griffin had gone into the equipment room. "And how do you get to play racketball on a Sunday? I thought the Y was closed on Sundays."

"Dan works for my dad."

"He what?"

"My dad is the new director of the YMCA."

"Big Bob is your dad?!" Barry could hardly contain his awe.

"Yeah," Ben said simply. "He said if I ever wanted to bring some friends to employee night—every Sunday night—I could. Since all my friends are in Pennsylvania maybe you guys would want to come in their place sometime. Let me know. We almost have the run of the place by ourselves. It's great. Like I said, think about it and let me know."

"I've thought. I'm coming," Rick said.

"Me too," said Allen.

"That makes it unanimous," Barry said.

"All right," Ben said. "Be here at 7:00 Sunday night. See ya!"

The three boys watched him trot down the floor, stop at the corner of the court, turn and toss a high looping shot neatly through the center of the rim. He turned and saw the others watching, then called out, "I forget if that's six or seven in a row." Then Ben laughed, waved, and made his exit.

Barry's prayer: Lord, where would I be today if I had to force people to be my friends like we tried to force Ben? Even worse, what if I thought I had to force you to like me? You make friendship easy. Help me to learn from you. Amen.

Action idea: This is an easy one to do after reading the story. Instead of waiting for someone you want to be your friend to join you, do something friendly to that other person. Watch the results when you are ready to do things for others!

"Like cold water to a weary soul
is good news from a distant land."
—Proverbs 25:25

•

"He told me so much about his country
that I sometimes dream that I am there with him."
—Rob

1st Prize:

Longest Distance Friendship

Robert—Rob—was a natural to win in this category since he was the only person who regularly wrote to someone living overseas. Rob never actually told this story to the class. But he did bring letters from home that told the story for him.

•

Dear Samueli,   May 3

Did you get back to Ethiopia yet? Dumb question! If you are reading this letter, then I guess you would have to be home by now. I'm not the world's best letter writer. In fact, I have only written thank-you's at Christmastime, but I am going to write once a month if I can keep it up.

Please excuse the mess on the back of this page. I am going to keep a copy of every letter I send, so

I am learning how to use carbon paper. Well, I got the carbon paper in the typewriter backwards so you now have ink on both sides of this page. Sorry.

Is Ethiopia as hot as you thought it would be this time of year? Is it still as dry as you thought it would be?

How was your plane ride? Did you enjoy sitting with the foreign exchange student we met at the airport?

Now that you are gone I am back to not having a brother, only two sisters.

Mom and dad said to say hi. Cissy and Jessica say hi too.

Keep in touch. You don't have to write once a month like me, but once in a while would be nice.

Your friend,
Rob

●

Dear Sámueli,   June 10

We haven't heard if you got home safely yet, but I suppose mail takes a long time to get back to the States. Anyway, if you had any real problems the people in charge of the foreign exchange program at our school would have heard something. So we are sure you are fine.

I am sending this letter in a card that your friends at school wanted me to send for your birthday. They all signed the card and wrote dumb things. I think they miss you.

Nobody knows who will be the place kicker this fall now that you are gone. Are you playing soccer at your own school again? I forgot, your school had to close on account of your town not having enough food. If enough people move back to town (if the town gets all the food it needs), will they try to find a teacher again? If your school doesn't open again, how will you graduate from high school? And if you don't graduate from high school, how would you ever come back to the States to go to college like you said?

Did your mom ever find anyone to buy the cattle? Or did they die or get stolen first like she thought they would?

Boy, is my letter getting depressing! I think that will be all for now.

Your friend,
Rob

●

Dear Samueli,   Fourth of July

Mom and dad are getting worried about you. We haven't heard from you yet. If you are getting my letters, please write a short letter to them. Thank you.

It's the Fourth of July! We were talking this afternoon how last year you had your first hot dog on the Fourth of July. We think that's when you became a real American. (Ha, ha!) Do your people have a day when they celebrate being free? Maybe not. I remember you talking about how things are not always as free as people would want.

This is going to be just a short letter, mainly to tell you to write to mom and dad when you get a chance. Dad jokes that now that you are gone we finally have the use of both cars again. He is thinking of trying to send a bicycle to Ethiopia for you to use. I know that there aren't even too many of those and almost no cars near where you live. He wants to know if you think it might get to you or if you think it would probably be stolen on the way. Let us know. We won't send anything until you say so. We wouldn't buy a fancy one—maybe a bike with only one gear that would be easy to fix.

Mom and dad said to say hi to your mom and brothers and sisters. Did your dad get back yet? Does anybody know where he is?

Your friend,
Rob

•

Dear Robbie and family,   June 15

I am home at last!

It took some extra days because I had to talk with our own foreign exchange program organizers and with the government about my year in the United States. Then I found that it was very hard to travel home, harder even than last year. I took a bus almost halfway, but then I walked the rest of the way home (almost 100 kilometers). That took almost a week. I stayed with people who are friends of my family on the way, but one night I had to sleep with just a fire under the stars. In the middle of the night a pack of dogs came too close to me so I stayed awake with a large fire until the sun came up.

I can't tell you all the details, but my family is not all well. When my youngest brother is well enough to travel we will also leave the town. So many have gone away already. My father is still gone. He went to find help from some relatives in the north but has been gone for six months now. We hope he will return before we have to move. How will he know where we went?

I never thought life would be like this. At one time my family was one of the richest in the area — we had many cattle. Maybe I should have stayed here with them this past year. But then I would never have met my American family. My mother is happy I had such a good year, though. I tell my family about you all the time, just like I used to talk to you about them.

Say hi for me to mom, dad, Cissy, Jessica, and to the guys on the track team. Did they get to go to state? Would I have gone to state with my best time in the mile? I have kept up with my running, but only to get water every day. Since the water truck no longer is running, I must travel five miles each way. (Of course, I cannot run when the buckets are full.)

I love you all. God loves you too.

Your brother,
Samueli

●

Dear Samueli,   August 21

We got your letter! We are glad you got home in one piece.

We are sorry to hear your father has not returned. If you move, please send us your new address. Your father has our address and might write to us, hoping we know where you are. Also, we want to keep track of you.

School is going to start soon. Don't tell mom and dad I said so, but I'm glad it is starting again. I'll be in the seventh grade. Mrs. Shade will be my teacher. I guess she will be OK. She can't be as bad as you-know-who! He was a bear.

Do you really have wild dogs in your country? Wow! Did you ever see Mrs. Cox's Doberman? If he were loose like those you met, even a fire wouldn't have helped you.

The track team did go to the state tournaments. At least, seven of the guys went. If you had been here it would have been eight. And if you had taken two seconds off your best meet time like you did that day in practice, dad says you would have taken third! The coach told me he hopes we get another runner from Ethiopia if they're all as good as you.

Remember, you have a home with us if you can come back here to go to college. Mom and dad were

not kidding when they said you could stay here all
four years.

>Your brother,
>Robbie

●

Dear Robbie and family,   August 13
  This will be my last letter to you for a while. We
are moving. I don't know where we are going.
  Good news! My father returned from the north
and my brother is now well enough to travel. Once
again my family is whole. We are lucky. So many
families have lost people to disease and hunger,
though the hunger is not quite as bad now as it used
to be. Living here is just too hard. It will be easier
in a refugee camp to find food and water every day.
I know it will be crowded, though.
  Please do not write anything about conversations
we may have had when I was in your country. Our
mail here is not always private. I am referring to
what you said at the end of the second paragraph in
your letter of July 4th.
  Do not send a bicycle or any other gifts until we
are settled. That may be a while. Is there a time for
me in the future to see you again and to go to college?
My mother and father on both sides of the ocean are
saying yes, so I have hope.
  Right now I am very busy since I am the oldest
boy of this family of eight. I will think about college
some other year.

Robbie, I remember the many good talks we had while we were brothers (and still are!). You helped me to learn so many things. I know that you will be 12 years old soon. In your country many do not think you are grown up until you are a teenager. But in my country you would already be thought of as grown up and ready to be married soon. So, from one man to another, I thank you for being such a good friend to me.

Your brother,
Samueli

Samueli's prayer: Dearest Lord Jesus, you said once that you are the bread of the world. Thank you for saying such a wonderful thing and for letting me meet my American family who believes that too. People like that give so much food to my people in Africa. They are your hands, aren't they? Amen.

Action idea: What are people in your church doing to get food and money to people like Samueli and his family in Africa? Give what you can to help. If your church is not yet doing anything, your gift might help get something started!

"If anyone wants to be first, he must be
the very last, and the servant of all."
—Mark 9:35b

•

*"If I had won in this category the way I wanted
to win, I would have lost!"*
—Chris

1st Prize:

Newest Friendship

Almost every morning during Friendship Olympics time somebody would tell a quick story about a new friendship that had begun. At first it seemed that the class was just a friendly group of boys and girls. But soon it was discovered that not all of the new friendships were accidental.

Julie had started visiting houses in the neighborhood trying to sell newspaper subscriptions for her paper route. She just took more time with each person than she usually did. Sometimes a new friendship would be the result.

Ben used his "in" at the YMCA—his dad is the new director, you know—to meet people who were joining for the first time. Friendships start very naturally in the midst of sports, he discovered.

Adrian continued her visits at the nursing home even after her friend, Stuart, had died. Many people there were happy to enter into new friendships.

Everybody had plans on how they might win in the Newest Friendship category of the Friendship Olympics.

But Mrs. Shade had her own ideas about the competition and the way it was developing.

"It looks like you kids have found more and more ways to get to know people," she said. "I am happy for that. But it seems that there will always be just one more friend around the corner for each of you. I suggest that we make Friday of this week the day to decide once and for all who wins in the Newest Friendship category."

Everybody has an equal chance that way, I suppose, thought Chris. *But they don't know that I have an extra advantage. On Thursday night the Robertsons from Toledo are coming to visit. Mom and dad went to college with the Robertsons back in the Dark Ages, but I've never met them. And they have this kid named Bertram Robertson the Third. The timing couldn't be better. Bertram, here I come.*

Bertram was an eighth grader, a *big* eighth grader. And he didn't wear glasses and study science projects in his spare time like you might think someone named Bertram Robertson III might do.

"Do you have a bowling alley near here?" Bertram asked when he and Chris were alone for the first time. "Let's go hustle quarters at the bowling alley."

"It's on the other end of town," Chris replied, "and what do you mean, 'hustle'?"

"Or we could hustle chicks at the roller rink."

"That's next to the bowling alley," Chris said. "What do you mean, 'hustle'?"

"You know—hustle! Like hustling cigarettes at the store. You got a store near here?"

Chris didn't like the sound of the word *hustle,* so he lied: "No, we don't even have a store near us."

"So what do you have to do around here?"

No hustling, that's for sure, Chris thought. *It's going to be a long night.*

It was.

At breakfast Chris's mother said, "Bertram says he'll go with you to school this morning, Christopher."

"I'll pretend I flunked back to seventh grade for a day," Bertram said.

Not a bad idea, Chris thought.

"You both will have to hustle, though," she said.

Chris looked up sharply and caught Bertram grinning at him.

"We will, Mrs. Felton, we will," Bertram said.

Five minutes and two blocks later, Chris and Bertram were crossing Pelter Avenue when Bertram spotted Sunshine Grocery Store.

"I thought you said there wasn't a store near you," he said.

"I guess this is kind of near," Chris said, "but not as near as it could be. Anyway, I don't think we should hustle cigarettes. We don't have time."

63

"I don't want to hustle cigarettes," Bertram replied.

"Good."

"I want to hustle buns."

"Buns?"

"You know, like Twinkies, Ho-Hos, cupcakes, and stuff like that for breakfast."

"But we just had breakfast."

"Not this kind."

"But I don't have any money."

"Don't need it."

"You have enough for both of us?" Chris said hopefully.

"You kidding? We're going to *hustle* the buns."

Just then a car stopped next to the curb where they were talking.

"Can you boys tell me where Kingston Middle School is?" a man asked.

"You're really close," Chris returned. "Just keep on to the next intersection, take a right and you will see the school on your left."

"Thanks a lot."

"That's all right."

When the car had gone, Chris turned to Bertram and thought to himself, *Friendship Olympics or no Friendship Olympics, I'm not going to hustle buns from the old lady in Sunshine Grocery Store. After getting him for a friend, I wouldn't deserve to win anything.*

"Sorry, Bertram, but I'm not going with you. And if you're not coming with me right now, I'm not waiting."

"You're a squirt, you know that?" Bertram called after Chris.

Chris kept his eyes straight ahead all the way to school.

As he cut through the parking lot he saw the man he had given directions to getting out of his car.

"You again—" the man said to Chris. "Now will you tell me where the principal's office is?"

"Sure, follow me," Chris replied.

"Did your friend get lost?"

"Him? I *thought* he was my newest friend, but I guess I was wrong. Yes, I guess he got lost."

"I didn't mean that literally "

"I know what you meant. The principal's office is just inside that door and to the right."

"Thanks again."

"Sure. See you later."

"Maybe," the man replied.

Chris found his way to his locker, nodding at a friend here and there. He opened the lock, took out his books, hung up his jacket and turned to go to his classroom.

He stopped for a drink at the fountain next to the music room, then looked up to see the same man from the car and the principal's office.

"Third time is the charm," the man said. "Can you show me to Room 112?"

"Going there myself," Chris said. "It's my classroom."

"Then you know Mrs. Shade," he said.

"Sure."

"Well, I'm Mr. Shade. What's your name?"

"Chris—Chris Felton."

"Glad to meet you, Chris."

"Same here."

"I hate to admit it, but I haven't even visited my wife's school since she started working here last fall. We don't live in town, you know. And I'm on the road all week traveling."

"I see. Here's the room."

"Thanks again, Chris, for everything."

Chris was early, but he took his seat and wondered, as he watched the other kids come in, where Bertram Robertson III was. His newest "friend." What a joke.

By the time class started, Bertram hadn't shown up. Chris wasn't surprised. *Probably caught "hustling buns,"* Chris thought.

"Class," Mrs. Shade announced, "before we get going on the Friendship Olympics for today—"

She waved down several hands that were already raised.

"Before I call on anyone, I want to introduce my husband, Dennis Shade. Dennis took a day off just to come to be with us."

Mr. Shade stood near the teacher's chair, waved and said, "I've heard a lot about this class. It'll be good to get to know you. I've already met a new friend, Chris Felton over there. He gave me good directions three times this morning."

The class groaned loudly.

Chris grinned.

Mr. Shade exclaimed, "What did I say?"

Chris's prayer: I would have done almost anything, Lord, just to win one of these Friendship Olympics events. But anyone who wants you to "sell out" on what you believe is right isn't going to be much of a friend, so I'm glad that it didn't work out with Bertram. I think I learned more from failing with him than I did in winning with Mr. Shade. Amen.

Action idea: Read this story again, and note some of the ways that the kids tried to find new friends. Put a + next to the ones that you think are good ideas and put a − next to those that aren't as good.

"For when I am weak, then I am strong."
—2 Corinthians 12:10b

•

*"A camping lantern shines brighter under pressure.
So does our friendship."*
—Jeremy

1st Prize:

Strongest Friendship

"We fight like cats and dogs sometimes," Rob said with his arm draped around Jeremy.

"Doesn't sound like the Strongest Friendship, Rob," Barry said. "You'd better sit down."

"Just wait," he continued, "it gets worse."

"He plays jokes on me," Jeremy said.

"Like the time when—"

"Do you boys know that you said your story was about the Strongest Friendship?" Mrs. Shade asked.

"We have a different way of looking at it, I guess," Rob said.

"Well, if you want to continue with your story, go ahead," she said.

"One time, on a Monday night, Rob stayed over at my house," Jeremy said. "His parents were out of town for the night and I have two beds in my room, so it was easy to have him stay over."

69

"So I changed all the—"

"This story is mine, Rob," Jeremy said. "Be quiet. Anyway, Rob changed all the clocks in the house ahead an hour—"

"—and watches—"

"—except for my dad's watch."

"He wears his watch to bed—can you believe it?" Rob said.

"So we all got up at 7:00 to get ready for school and work—"

"—except it was really 6:00—"

"Anyway," Jeremy said, "Rob never told anyone about it before we were all off to work and school. I remember my mother kept saying, "Gosh, it's dark out for 7:00 in the morning.""

"We waited for quite a while before anyone even came to open the school doors," Rob said.

In the back of the classroom Ben scratched his head and said, "I still don't know why you are telling this as a story about the Strongest Friendship."

"Hang on," Rob said. "We're coming to that."

"Then there was the time that Rob and I were riding with my brother in my brother's car," Jeremy continued.

"He was going to teach me a lesson for playing the tricks with the clocks—"

"So while Rob was sitting in the middle of the front seat with me on the right," Jeremy said, "just as we were about to pass the school ground, I ducked down. It looked like my brother was riding around with his girlfriend next to him, except it was really Rob. All kinds of people saw them."

"There's more," said Rob. "We've had food fights in the cafeteria—everybody knows that. And we've gotten each other lost on Boy Scout camp-outs. We have done every weird thing to each other that we could think of."

"And most of it isn't funny at all while it's happening," Jeremy continued.

"No, we get really *mad* at each other."

"Like Rob said at the beginning, sometimes we fight like cats and dogs. Our parents say that all the time."

"I give up," Ben said from his desk. "What does your story have to do with a Strongest Friendship?"

"Good question. I'm glad you asked that question," Rob said. "Tell 'em, Jeremy."

"It's like this," Jeremy said. "Barry and Allen and Rick told how they have gone camping with each other—all three families together—since they were all in first grade. It's easy to be friends when you have such a nice background as that."

"Adrian's and Julie's Strongest Friendship story was about how they've never had a fight or disagreement about anything," Rob said. "It's easy to be friends when you never have an argument."

"But we're just plain mean to each other sometimes," Jeremy said. "Get it?"

"I don't think so," Ben answered for the whole class. "Do you think it's good to be mean to each other?"

"Of course not," Rob said. "That's the whole point. Look at all the stuff we both have to put up with from each other. Can you believe we're still friends?"

"I can't," Jeremy said.

"I can't either," Rob agreed. "What kind of a friendship can survive even the tough test we put each other through?"

"Only the Strongest Friendship, of course!" Jeremy said right on cue.

"A friendship isn't necessarily strong just because it's been around for a long time," Rob said with a smile. "It's strong if it can stand up through a lot of hard times."

"Now I'm in real trouble," Ben said.

"Don't you understand?" Rob asked.

"The problem isn't that I don't understand; the problem is I'm starting to agree with your weird way of seeing things."

"Who's weird?" Rob asked, pointing to Jeremy. "Him?"

"Look who's talking—" Jeremy said as they sat down.

Rob's prayer: God, we may have acted dumb in front of the class today, but when they told us we won we were so happy. Who makes the glue that holds friendships like Jeremy's and mine together?

Action idea: Go to the nearest park and find an object that reminds you of a friend who is sometimes hard to get along with. Then give the object to your friend and tell him or her why you chose it. (For example, a pinecone may get sticky sometimes, but it's also packed with seeds that can grow beautiful trees.)

74

"Finally, brothers, whatever is true,
whatever is noble, whatever is right,
whatever is pure, whatever is lovely,
whatever is admirable—if anything is excellent
or praiseworthy—think about such things."
—Philippians 4:8

•

*"Take my word for it;
you don't want to sleep with a bear."*
—Danny

1st Prize:

Strongest Friendship

"Upbeat Friendship"

"This is most unusual," Mrs. Shade told Danny. "We already had a winner in this category last week. Everybody had an equal chance to share stories of strong friendships."

"I know," he replied, "but Steve and I have been thinking since then. Do you have to go through all kinds of bad times together like Rob and Jeremy did in order to have a strong friendship?"

"But the Friendship Olympics can only have one winner in each category," she replied. "Isn't that right, class?"

Nobody answered right away.

Finally, Adrian said, "When I am in an ice-skating competition there can be a tie. Why not in the Friendship Olympics?"

"Sure," Jeremy said. "If they have a good story about a strong friendship, as good as the one about Rob and me, they should have a chance to tie if they can."

"I guess the real Olympics has ties, don't they?" Mrs. Shade said. "All right. Let's see if a friendship of a different sort can be as strong as the one between Rob and Jeremy."

"I think last summer was the best time we have ever had together," Danny started.

"No doubt about it," Steve returned.

"So, we'll tell you about that, and maybe you can understand how friendships can be strong without going through all the tough things that Jeremy and Rob did."

"Our families went camping together in the Tetons," said Danny. "Those are mountains in Wyoming near Yellowstone."

"It was great!" Steve continued. "After we got set up at the campground, Danny and I went exploring. There were trails all over the place, some of them with hidden entrances that most people wouldn't ever know about."

"We hiked all over the place. We mapped out all the trails as best as we could, putting landmarks at the key places where they belonged on the map—things like big stumps, creeks, meadows—"

"Even a cave, if you crawled past some bushes," Steve said.

"We didn't go in it at first," Danny said. "We thought it was too dangerous."

"But one night at about 8:30 a ranger came driving along in her truck with two people in front and some other adults and kids in back. You could tell they were worried."

"They were looking for a six-year-old boy who had been playing hide-and-seek with some other kids earlier in the evening. No one could find him. They wanted to know if we had seen him."

"Nobody had," Steve said. "But then someone remembered that the lost boy had said he had the best hiding place—in a cave."

"And the ranger said, 'But there aren't any caves in this area. He must have been mistaken,' " Danny added.

"But Danny and I knew right away where the cave was because we had found it!" Steve exclaimed.

"So we told the ranger, and she asked if we could remember where it was."

"Ten minutes later we were all at the cave, and sure enough the boy was in there. He was sound asleep because it was such a cool place to be on a hot day."

"That was fun," Danny said. "We're better friends because we got to be heroes together in saving that dumb kid."

"Be careful about calling anyone dumb after what happened that night," Steve said quickly.

"Shhh—"

"Tell us the rest of the story!" the class eagerly said.

Steve ignored the jabbing in the ribs from Danny as he continued, "Well, Danny said that since he wasn't afraid of anything, we should both sleep out in the tent instead of in the camper with our families."

"Steeeeeve," Danny said under his breath.

"So we slept outside in our sleeping bags even though I was a little scared. Anyway, in the middle of the night, probably around 3:00 in the morning, this big, heavy thing comes and lies down outside of our tent. We both woke up right away."

"I could feel the big, furry body through the tent," Danny said, "and I could hear breathing so loud that I knew it wasn't someone playing a trick on us."

"We stayed awake for hours with this thing lying on the bottoms of our sleeping bags, trapping our legs."

"And we prayed."

"Boy, did we pray," Steve said.

"In the morning," Danny continued, "Steve's little sister came out of the trailer and whistled. And you know what? The animal got up and went over to her."

"What?!" exclaimed the class.

"It was a great big, drooling St. Bernard that was lost and just wanted some company for the night," Steve said with a grin.

Mrs. Shade said, "I thought you two were going to tell us how your friendship is based on so many good times. But it sounds like you had some serious things happen to you."

"I guess we've had both good and bad times, but we like to remember the good times best," Steve said.

"And some of the bad times end up sounding like good times after you have a while to think about them," Danny added.

Danny's prayer: *Lord, lots of our good times together have been mixed in with the hard times when we've been scared or have argued. Help us to learn from the hard times and grow from them. And help the good times to build good friendships. Amen.*

Action idea: Press your hands together tightly. Now push them into each other as hard as you can. You can feel the muscles in your arms and shoulders tense up. This is a conflict that will make you stronger if you do this exercize several times every day. In the same way, friends who go through challenging experiences together can grow together.

"Better a meal of vegetables where there is love
than a fattened calf with hatred."
—Proverbs 15:17

●

*"Do I love Lisa? That's a good question.
No comment."*
—Michael

1st Prize:

Most Secret Friendship

"It's called a Box Lunch Service Project," the
youth director at the church said to the junior high
kids. "It's a fun way for you to get to know each
other and do something to help other people at the
same time."

"I don't get it, Peter," someone called from the
back of the church basement.

"One more time then," he said. "I am about to
draw names out of these hats. There's a boys' hat
and a girls' hat. Chris will write the names down in
pairs so a girl and boy make up a team. As teams,
you will have to sit down before you leave this evening and decide who will do the service project and
who will make the box lunches for next Saturday.
The one who does the service project must do it

before next Saturday, and the one who makes the box lunches must have them ready for the picnic next Saturday. Be here at noon. Any questions?"

"Do the girls have to do all the cooking?" a girl asked.

"I'd suggest that the best cook do the cooking and the other person do the service project."

"Can we bring anything we want in the box lunches?" Chris asked from the chalkboard in front. "How about chocolate-covered french fries?"

"There are no rules about what you bring for the picnic, but I suggest that if you want to make friends with the person you cook for, bring something good."

Michael had an uneasy feeling about the whole thing. As he looked from face to face at the girls, he tried to imagine having fun with any of them on this—this picnic date. It was a date, wasn't it? His first. And maybe his last if it didn't work out.

Peter, the youth worker, called out the names: "Danny . . . and . . . Robin, Ben . . . and . . . Julie, Rob . . . and . . . Jenny, Barry . . . and . . . Adrian . . . ."

With each pair of names came the giggles and outright laughter that Michael expected. People nudged and punched each other in the arm when names were called.

Then Michael heard, "Michael . . . and . . . Lisa."

Without thinking, he turned to the back of the room where he knew Lisa would be sitting. She met his gaze, then looked down.

Lisa was shy. She hardly ever raised her hand in class; she never volunteered for anything in the church youth group; and she had trouble looking someone straight in the eye.

The pairing up of boys and girls continued until both hats were empty.

Lisa! Michael thought. *She is probably the only girl that I don't know very well.*

He turned slightly to catch her staring at him, but she looked down again right away.

"Get together with your partner now and I will come around and give each team a service project," said Peter. "Remember, you must choose tonight who will do the service project and who will bring box lunches next Saturday. You may leave when you have done this. See you next Saturday!"

Lisa waited for Michael to come over to her. When he got there he didn't know what to say so he just sat down against the wall next to her and waited for Peter to come with their assigned service project.

Peter handed an index card to Michael and said, "You have one of the toughest ones. Mrs. Wilkins needs her yard mowed because Mr. Wilkins is in the hospital. She doesn't know of anyone in the neighborhood who can help. It's a toughie because she also needs the empty lot next to their house mowed, but—" and Peter got down close to them so he could whisper, "—she is the only one who has insisted on paying whoever helps her. She won't let you help her for nothing."

After looking at Lisa, who nodded, Michael said, "OK."

"You can ask for a different one if you want," Peter said.

"No," Michael said, "this one is fine. I've done a lot of mowing."

After Peter had gone, Lisa said, "I think I should do the mowing. Mrs. Wilkins lives less than a block from me and a long ways from you."

Peter turned to look at Lisa, but she turned away.

"—if that's all right with you," she said.

"Sure, if you think you can—"

"—it's no problem to—"

"I guess I'll do the food, so—"

"Anything is fine with me—"

"Me too," Michael said. "Do you want help with the mowing, then?"

"I have all week to do it," Lisa replied. "And I'll split the money with you if you are doing the food for Saturday. . . ."

"But it won't be any good," Michael said as he shuffled to his feet. "I mean, I'll make it as good as I can, but—"

"OK, well, I guess I'll see you next Saturday then," Lisa said with a smile straight into Michael's face.

Michael looked down this time, then said, "Bye."

All week long Lisa seemed to be around every corner, Michael thought. They always exchanged smiles, but Michael could never think of anything to say except, "How is the mowing going?" Michael couldn't believe that for years he had hardly noticed Lisa at all. Now he found himself thinking about her even when she wasn't around.

And Michael thought more and more about food. What should he bring for the picnic?

On Wednesday evening Michael's dad made his famous fried chicken with enough to spare for Michael and Lisa to eat cold on Saturday. After deciding that, the rest came easy. Fancy chips with dip, a monster dill pickle for each, strawberry soda from the health food store—the kind that was thick with real strawberries, and some chocolate mints for dessert.

"Don't forget to make the picnic look as great as it tastes," his mother told him. She helped to pull together some of the necessary items into a real picnic basket and took Michael to the store to pick out the needed food items, so Michael found himself ready for the picnic already on Friday.

"How is the mowing going?" he asked Lisa on Friday afternoon.

"I'm done!" she said with a smile. "Have you started fixing things for the picnic yet?"

"I'm done too," he said.

"Are we having something good?"

Michael tried not to look too proud when he said, "You'll just have to wait and see." Secretly, he knew it would be the best-looking and best-tasting picnic lunch of all.

At 11:45 A.M. on Saturday morning, Michael got the picnic basket from the front closet, then went to the refrigerator to pack the chicken in with the forks and napkins and other stuff his mother had already helped him pack.

No chicken.

"Where's the chicken?" he shouted at the ceiling.

His father entered the kitchen.

"It's in the freezer where I put it on Wednesday," he said, "unless you've pulled it out."

"It's frozen?"

"I didn't know if it would keep well enough in the refrigerator."

"It's rock solid, isn't it?"

"Here," his dad said taking the chicken from the freezer and popping it into the microwave oven. "It will be thawed out in no time if we set it on high."

"That's what I've got: no time!" Michael said as he threw open the coat closet and fished out his jacket.

"That's going to have to do, dad," Michael said. "Maybe it will thaw out the rest of the way before we have to eat it."

"Don't forget the sodas," his father said as Michael headed out the door. He returned for the strawberry sodas, then ran out of the house.

Lisa was waiting for him with the others at the big bell in the park.

"Find your own spot to eat, now, then come back here when I ring the bell."

"Over here," Lisa said. "I already picked out the best spot in the park. Can I carry anything? It looks wonderful already in that great basket."

She led the way toward the river, then stepped down by way of some tree roots onto a lower grassy area that was flat.

"Be careful for the—" she began.

Michael slipped on one of the roots, but caught his footing and the basket at the last possible moment. It was very dramatic. But he realized that in the noise of the near-fall he had heard two bottles crack together.

Strawberry soda leaked through the bottom strips of the basket.

"Are you hurt?" Lisa asked. "Don't worry about the mess. I wasn't thirsty anyway."

Michael realized that Lisa had lost her shyness rather quickly. He knew he was seeing a side of her that none of the boys had ever seen before.

She seems so happy. I think she likes me. She's pretty—but I'm not going to tell anyone I think so. Why didn't I notice before?

As they spread out the blanket on the ground, Michael realized that she had to have the longest hair in the class, and the prettiest.

They touched hands in the basket as they were both unpacking the items and Michael wondered if she had noticed that he had noticed that they had touched hands.

In the unpacking of the basket it soon became clear that all was not right. The sodas had broken all over everything since they had been on top. The chips and pickles had been forgotten in a bag in the refrigerator during the worry about the chicken. And the chocolate mints, as Michael would find out later, had been snitched by his younger brother.

As they unpacked the forks and knives and spoons and plates and napkins and napkin rings and soaked placemats and toothpicks and a plastic flower in a plastic vase and even a bag for the chicken bones, Lisa said, "Well, the chicken sure looks good."

Michael dropped a piece on his plate with a noise that sounded like glass on glass. They would never get to the bones in order to use the bag. There was no picnic lunch.

A week ago, Michael wouldn't have cared much. But Lisa had changed, he thought. She was more open. And maybe Michael had changed too.

"Michael," Lisa said quietly, "let's not tell anyone. Then, after everyone else goes home at 2:00, we will take the $10.00 that Mrs. Wilkins gave me and have anything we want on the menu at Dorothy's Cafe. How about it?"

Michael wondered why he wasn't embarrassed over the whole bothersome lunch, but he was quick to say, "Sure. It'll be our secret."

As it turned out, nobody in their class at school heard about the malts and burgers and pie at Dorothy's Cafe. It also happened that Michael and Lisa didn't bother to enter this story in the category of Most Secret Friendship. Such secrets are not to be told easily.

But Michael and Lisa—with their friendship that would last and grow for a long time—knew that they could have had first prize if they had wanted it.

Lisa's prayer: Dear God, you know what I feel like every time I see Michael. Right now I can't tell anyone else about him, but I have to talk with someone so I'm glad I can talk to you anytime. He's special. So are you, God. Amen.

Action idea: Do you have a secret friendship? If you do and you haven't even told that person about it, you can always talk to God about that friendship. Tell God about it.

"... and your Father, who sees what is done
in secret, will reward you."
—Matthew 6:18b

•

*"I don't mean to lie, but sometimes the truth
just isn't interesting enough."*
—Laine

1st Prize:

Most Secret Friendship

"Storybook Secret"

The story of Michael and Lisa never became a
part of the Friendship Olympics. It remained their
secret.

However, one story stood out above the others that
were actually entered in that category. That was because it was not just a story about one person; it was
a story about the whole class.

•

Laine looked straight into the eyes of each of the
four boys in front of him as he said: "And I not only
learned to drive this summer, but I even turned a
corner at 45 miles an hour while steering with my
knees."

The others looked unimpressed.

"Really!" Laine emphasized. "I know you don't believe me, but it's true," he said with feeling.

"If you were driving with your knees," Chris said, "how could you have your foot on the brake at the same time?"

"I didn't use the brake because I wasn't trying to slow down. I was trying to take the corner as fast as I could."

"Weren't you afraid of an accident?" Chris continued.

"Well, I was in my cousin's dune buggy with a roll bar on top so even if I went too fast—"

"Yes, but 45 miles an hour?!" Danny spouted.

"Have you ever driven a dune buggy!" Laine demanded.

"I haven't even seen one except on TV," Danny replied.

"Then don't make such a big deal about something you don't know anything about," he said.

Danny and the others were silent. They tossed more stones into the lake, one at a time. Gregory threw some big stones, trying very hard to sink a large, flat leaf 50 feet from the shore. On the fifth try the wet leaf was ripped to pieces. He turned and gave Laine a hard look, but he didn't say anything.

The next morning, Gregory was early to school. To kill time, he eased over to a group of girls at the chalkboard as they played "hangman" and talked to Laine.

". . . and I already have my name on the list to go up in the space shuttle once they open it to kids," Laine was saying. "So I suppose I'll be the first one from this class, or even from this town, to go into space. I wouldn't have known about it if it hadn't been for the science magazine that my dad gets. He's a space scientist—sort of."

"I thought he worked with computers," Elizabeth said snidely.

"He does," Laine replied. "It's just that sometimes he does things with his computer to help out NASA. He writes programs and things."

Gregory looked over Laine's shoulder from behind him and wiggled his eyebrows at the girls. They laughed. Laine turned and glared at Gregory.

"So what gives you the right to sneak up on a guy?" Laine asked.

"You're such an amazing guy with so many amazing stories, Laine, that I thought maybe you also have eyes in the back of your head. Maybe if you combed your hair differently in back, we could see if—"

"Don't make fun of me, Gregory," Laine said in return.

I don't like his tall stories, like he thinks he lives in a storybook or something, Gregory thought, *but if I pick on him the others will think I'm being too mean. Besides, if I wait, I'll bet he will get himself into trouble with his lies.*

"Sorry," Gregory heard himself say through tight lips.

The girls turned away from the two boys, seeming to be embarrassed at the exchange.

An hour later, Mrs. Shade addressed the class: "Tryouts for the musical will be after school today, as you know. The music teacher asked me to announce that they are looking for a piano player, too. There are teachers or parents who could play for the musical, but the music committee would rather go with a student if there is someone who plays well enough. I hope we have some volunteers."

Elizabeth's hand shot up quickly.

"Yes?"

"Mrs. Shade," she said, "Laine says he has studied piano since he was three years old and he has even won some contests."

Mrs. Shade turned her attention to Laine who was slumping in his chair.

"Is that true? Do you want to try it, Laine?"

"Sure, go ahead, Laine," Chris said.

"All right, Laine!" somebody else said.

Gregory held his breath. *This is what I've been waiting for,* he thought. *He'll be caught in a fib for sure.*

"I suppose I could try," Laine responded.

What? He didn't back down?

"Then you are to go to the tryouts after school as well," Mrs. Shade said. "I didn't know we had such a musician in our class."

The day just didn't go fast enough for Gregory. He felt happier and happier as the final bell approached. Laine, on the other hand, seemed to get more and more pale.

That's it! Gregory thought. *He's making himself sick so he will have to go home before the tryout.*

But the final bell rang and Laine made his way to the auditorium with all the others.

A full hour passed as kids of all ages read or sang the same few lines. Normally, Gregory would have been bored. But he spent his time looking at Laine who was sitting a few rows ahead and trying to read his mind.

Finally, the music teacher turned to the audience and said, "I don't suppose anyone is here to try out for the piano part."

Laine shrunk in his seat a bit as he raised his hand slowly.

"Wonderful! Can you come down here and play for us?"

Laine looked as if he was on his way to a funeral.

He'll throw up before he gets there, Gregory thought to himself.

"Here's the opening number that I was just playing for all the young singers. Try this," the music teacher said.

"Can I just play a piece from memory, and then take this book home to study for later?" Laine asked.

"You can play something from memory?" The teacher clearly looked pleased. "By all means—"

Laine played. Beautifully. With great feeling and flying fingers.

Gregory was dumbfounded. *If he's that good, why has he had such a sour face since he found out about the tryouts this morning?*

95

When he was finished, the auditorium erupted with applause. People who were on their way out had stopped to listen. The music teacher actually shook Laine's hand after she gave him the music book.

Gregory waited for Laine outside the auditorium.

"That was some playing you did back there," Gregory said as he fell into step next to Laine.

Laine looked like he was trying to remember something.

Finally he said, "I'm a fake."

"What?" Gregory asked with surprise.

"I'm not as good a piano player as everyone thinks."

"But we all heard you!"

"You heard me play a recital piece in the key of C that I had worked on for two years. It sounds hard, but it's easy and it's the only thing I can play."

Gregory didn't know what to say.

"I don't read music very well and I can't play in five flats which is what most of this music is," Laine said, holding up the music book the teacher had just given him.

Gregory still didn't know what to say.

"Most of what I say has a grain of truth to it," Laine continued, "but I usually make things sound better than they really are."

"Why do you think you have to do that, Laine?" Gregory finally said.

Laine didn't even have to think about his answer. "To make friends," he said.

"Hey, Laine, I'm more ready to be a friend of yours now that you're playing straight with me than I was when you were making things up."

"Really?"

"If you talk to the class like you're talking to me now, I think you will find that you really have lots of secret friends who want to like you. Besides, Laine, I wouldn't lie about a thing like that!"

Laine's prayer: I'm sorry, I'm sorry, I'm sorry. I hope you can forgive me, God, when I make things up all the time. I hope I haven't hurt anybody by doing that. Help me to quit. I think I feel freer already. Thanks, God. Amen.

Action idea: Make a list of all the times you can remember when you lied. If you like, write down just the first letter of each word. For example, "I lied when my parents asked me where I went" becomes "ILWMPAMWIW." Nobody but you will know what it means. Then, find a safe way to destroy the list as a way of asking God to forgive you. Finally, look up 1 John 1:9.

"He will take pity on the weak and the needy
and save the needy from death."
—Psalm 72:13

•

"Elizabeth almost killed us all on this one. Whew!"
—*Bill*

1st Prize:

Most Friends

The popularity contest was on.

Everybody knew that to win in the Most Friends category would be one of the highlights of the Friendship Olympics, maybe second only to the Decathlon of Friendship. In the real Olympics the person who won the 100 meter sprint was named "World's Fastest Human." Well, to Mrs. Shade's seventh grade class, the person who had the most friends would probably be called Mr. or Miss Popularity.

Bill ruled himself out of the race right from the start.

"I'm just not in the same league as most of the other kids," he told his father one night at supper. "I won't enter a story for this one."

"I don't blame you," his father replied as he cleared the table.

Thursday was the night that Bill actually loved doing the dishes. It was a special time for him to spend with his dad. His mother went to church choir practice at 6:30 and he knew his dad always kept the evening clear to be with him.

"I don't have that many friends," Bill said with a sigh.

"I liked this idea of your Olympics up 'til now," said his father. "The other categories have sounded fun, but this one really puts you kids on the spot. I'll have to talk with Mrs. Shade."

"Oh, dad—please don't."

"Someone should."

"Not this time," Bill said. "It's too embarrassing."

They worked in the kitchen in silence.

"Who do you think is going to win?" his father asked.

"I guess that depends on who can come up with the longest list," Bill answered.

"Lists? You're kidding."

•

"Let me see yours," Elizabeth said curtly.

Jean pulled a computer sheet out of her notebook and handed it to Elizabeth.

"Hmmm—computerized," she said, scanning the list of Jean's friends.

"Now let's see yours," Jean suggested.

"Sorry," Elizabeth said. "All's fair in love and war. I was just checking to see if I left anybody out."

"Oh, you—" Jean sputtered.

"But I have all those people on my own list already. Except for your cousin Albert from the farm. You'd better check that one out, Jean. I don't think cousins count—especially your cousin Albert."

"You are such a pain," Jean shouted loudly at Elizabeth as she huffed away, meeting Bill across the classroom. "Can you believe that?" Jean asked him. "Did you hear that girl?"

"I heard," he replied. "She's *your* friend, not mine."

"Make a bet?" With that, Jean pulled a pen out of the nearest desk and angrily crossed Elizabeth's name from her computer printout.

"You'll probably lose by just one name now," Bill said with a chuckle.

"I don't care," she said in return. "After what she just did to me, I'd do anything to see Elizabeth lose."

"Anything?" Bill asked with a more serious tone.

"Anything!"

"I'll remember that," he said as he walked away thoughtfully.

The half-hour sharing time every morning began to feel tense. Kids shared their stories in any category except Most Friends, but they all knew what was really on everybody else's mind. More than half the kids actually had lists of friends. Many who did not were gathering names in their heads, though they wouldn't have admitted it. Only Bill seemed not to care about the subject. He had fun by acting as a reporter during the day, interviewing all the others and giving a sports update on the scores as they developed. Ginny claimed 24 friends, Barry claimed 25, Allen claimed 37 (many from Boy Scouts), Ben claimed 41 (including some from Pennsylvania), Jean claimed 42, and on and on. Elizabeth was the only one who wouldn't tell Bill how long her list was. It only made the others more curious.

One morning, Mrs. Shade brought the subject out into the open.

"I know you kids have developed your own lists of friends for the Friendship Olympics. I hate to tell you this, but I am tempted to cancel the category of Most Friends. I think this whole thing is getting out of hand and can only end in people getting their feelings hurt."

A look of relief swept across the class. Many of the kids had already thought to themselves, *What if I list my friends and some of them refuse to allow their names to be on my list?*

"I like all the other categories," she continued, "but unless someone strongly objects, I am going to throw this one out."

Silence.

Then Elizabeth cleared her throat and said, "I'm sorry, but if we don't have this category there can't be a decathlon because a decathlon is based on ten events, not nine."

Most of the other kids groaned out loud.

Mrs. Shade was about to say something, but Bill raised his hand, asking to speak.

"Bill?"

"I want to enter a story in the category of Most Friends," he said simply.

Perhaps it was the amused expression in his eyes that made Mrs. Shade say, "All right. Proceed."

"Last summer I went to Europe with my family," he began. All eyes were on him. "Some of you remember my telling about our being robbed, right?"

Heads nodded.

"We were in church on Sunday morning at an English-speaking church. When we went back to the parking lot to get into our rented van, we found that the driver's window had been broken. All our cameras and film were gone, including film that we had taken in two weeks of traveling. Mom's purse was taken from under her seat. But the worst thing turned out to be that our passports were stolen from inside the camera bag.

"We were supposed to be on a flight back to the United States that night, but we couldn't get out of the country without passports. Mom and dad were supposed to be back at work the next day. And if we missed our flight we weren't sure we could get another one for days.

"The police drove us to the station after we had someone call for us and explain what had happened. There we were all fingerprinted and told to sit and wait.

"Pretty soon, somebody from the American embassy came to pick us up and take us to the embassy. He said he'd try to get us passports as quickly as possible, but because it was Sunday, there was really nobody at the embassy with the authority to do it.

"You know what? The ambassador came all the way from a dinner in another city when he heard about our problem. The ambassador himself!

"Not only that, but they took care of returning our rented van and they got us to the airport barely in time, with a police escort with lights and sirens going. A policeman met us there with all the film and mom's purse that had been found. We never did see the cameras or old passports again.

"I'm telling this story because we learned when all this happened that when a person needs help there are more friends willing to help than you ever thought existed! Even though there are some people who aren't friendly, I know that the number of my friends out there are easily in the millions. I just haven't met them all yet!"

"That's wonderful, Bill," Mrs. Shade said. "Does anybody have a story that they want to match against that one?"

Every eye turned to look at Elizabeth, who quickly looked down at her desk.

•

"How was school today?" Bill's dad asked him as he threw his books on the couch.

"Oh, the usual," he said, kicking his feet up on the coffee table. "I won in the Most Friends category." Bill tried to look casual, but he couldn't help smiling at his dad's look of surprise.

"How on earth?"

"What's more, Elizabeth came up to me after class and thanked me for doing it. She said she really didn't have much of a friendship list after all. She was just trying to psyche us all out. She invited the whole class to her birthday party next week, but she said she especially wanted me to come."

"Sounds like you made a new friend."

"Yup," Bill said with a pleased expression.

Elizabeth's prayer: I'm sorry, God, for teasing the other kids in my class. I never wanted to lie, but I wouldn't blame them if that's what they think I did. I want friends so badly that sometimes I scare them away. Teach me how to be a good friend. Amen.

Action idea: Think of one friend who has been a special blessing to you and thank that person for being such a good friend.

"You are my friends. . . ."
—John 15:14

•

"I wonder who wrote the letter?"
—Mrs. Shade

1st Prize:

The Decathlon of Friendship

"Class, as you know, this is the last day of our Friendship Olympics," Mrs. Shade said.

Boos and hisses accompanied smiles at some of the memories that the Olympics had brought.

"I know, it has been fun," she said. "Our last category is the Decathlon of Friendship."

"Nobody told a story in all of the 10 categories, though," Barry said. "I think we will have to throw this last one out."

"You have a point, Barry, but before we do that," Mrs. Shade continued, "I'd like to know who left this letter on my desk before school."

Everybody looked around for a hand to raise.

"No one owns up?"

Still no hand.

"What's in the letter, Mrs. Shade?" Rob asked.

"I think I should read it aloud, and then we'll take a vote on whether or not we should throw out the Decathlon of Friendship," she replied.

The class watched her with curiosity.

"Dear Seventh-Graders," she began. "I have been watching your Friendship Olympics for weeks now. I have enjoyed all the stories as much as you have. And I feel like a closer friend to each of you because of the Friendship Olympics.

"But we have this last category still to decide. Who wins the Decathlon of Friendship? Who shared the best collection of stories in *all 10 categories?* Nobody. At least, nobody shared a story out loud in all 10 categories. (I know that many stories were kept secret because some of the best things can't be shared that easily.)

"I think that only one person can win this final category: *my son!*"

The boys looked at each other and wondered whose parent would dare to send such a letter. And besides, except for Mr. Shade visiting one day, no one had visited the Friendship Olympics like this person claimed to have done.

"Let me give you my reasons, category by category, for nominating my son to win this final grand prize:

"*Most Improved Friendship:* My son has improved his friendships with almost all of you in the last year. Friendships improve mainly because someone cares a lot and wants them to improve. My son cares a lot about each of you.

"*Shortest Friendship:* My son is always getting to be friends with people just before they die. Adrian's friend, Stuart, was a friend of his for a very long time, but the lady in the room next to Stuart's who died the next month was a friend of my son's for just moments before she died.

"*Longest Distance Friendship:* My son has had friends as far away as the dark side of the moon. If you put your hand on a globe on the opposite side from where you live, my son has friends there too. Rob's friend, Samueli, is also a friend of my son.

"*Most Friends:* My son would never brag that he has the most friends, but the truth is that he has. Bill told an interesting story about how people all over the world might become friends of yours if you suddenly needed help. That is true. My son knows exactly how many people would actually give you that kind of help instead of taking advantage of you.

"*Most Giving Friendship:* My son understands giving even if it means giving his own blood like Greta did for Gregory. What a terrific story that was! My son gives in that way to his friends.

"*Most Secret Friendship:* My son doesn't need to keep any of his friendships secret, but he understands when some of his friends feel that they have to do so. He has friends you wouldn't believe!

"*Newest Friendship:* My son has made friends already this morning. There isn't a day that goes by that he doesn't make friends with someone new.

"*Strongest Friendship:* My son thinks the same way that Jeremy and Rob do—that a friendship is strongest if it can get through lots of tough times and still be there. No matter how tough it has gotten, my son has *never* given up a friendship.

"*Most Unlikely Friendship:* My son is as common as apple pie in a way, but he is also pretty amazing if I do say so myself. Spend time with him and people will think he's an odd one for you to hang out with— except the people who know him. They won't think your friendship is unlikely at all.

"Those are all my reasons for wanting my son to be in the running for the Decathlon of Friendship. Except for the one I almost forgot: *Most Time Spent with a Single Friend.* He wants to be *your* friend forever!" Mrs. Shade finished reading and put down the paper.

"But who signed the letter?" someone in the class asked.

"That's the strange part," said Mrs. Shade. "It wasn't signed."

"Well, if the person who wrote it wouldn't sign it, then we can't give the prize," suggested one of the boys.

"But it *was* a good story—" said Barry.

Mrs. Shade replied, "The Friendship Olympics was your idea to begin with, Barry. Maybe you should decide whether or not we award the prize."

"To who?" asked one of the girls.

Meanwhile, Barry sat in his desk with his best daydreamer look on his face. Suddenly he broke into a big grin.

"I'm not sure who wrote the letter," he said finally. "But I think I know who the story is about. And I think we should give him the prize."

"Who?" asked the class and Mrs. Shade at once.

"The Son of God. *Jesus.* He is the best friend of all!"

Somebody's prayer: God, I made it look like you wrote my story for the Decathlon of Friendship today. I hope you didn't mind. I just said the things that I thought you would write yourself. It's just that I learned so much about you during the Friendship Olympics that I thought there couldn't be anyone else who could win in the final category. I was right, wasn't I? I knew it!

Action idea: All of these categories of friendship tell about God's friendship with you. In a simple prayer, thank God for being your friend.